TWO TRUTHS AND A MYTH

PIRATES

SPOT THE MYTHS

by Carol Kim

CAPSTONE PRESS
a capstone imprint

T0009103

Published by Capstone Press, an imprint of Capstone
1710 Roe Crest Drive, North Mankato, Minnesota 56003
capstonepub.com

Library of Congress Cataloging-in-Publication Data
Names: Kim, Carol, author.
Title: Pirates : spot the myths / by Carol Kim.
Description: North Mankato, Minnesota : Capstone Press, 2024. | Series: Two truths and a myth | Includes bibliographical references and index. Audience: Ages 8-11 | Audience: Grades 4-6 | Summary: "Throughout history, people have told many stories about fearsome pirates on the high seas. But not all of them are true! Was walking the plank a common punishment that pirates used? Did pirates keep pets? Check out the stories. Then see if you can spot the myths!"— Provided by publisher.
Identifiers: LCCN 2023031090 (print) | LCCN 2023031091 (ebook) | ISBN 9781669062554 (hardcover) | ISBN 9781669062684 (paperback) | ISBN 9781669062585 (pdf) | ISBN 9781669062691 (epub) | ISBN 9781669062707 (kindle edition)
Subjects: LCSH: Pirates—Juvenile literature.
Classification: LCC G535 .K54 2024 (print) | LCC G535 (ebook) DDC 910.45—dc23/eng/20230705
LC record available at https://lccn.loc.gov/2023031090
LC ebook record available at https://lccn.loc.gov/2023031091

Editorial Credits
Editor: Carrie Sheely; Designer: Bobbie Nuytten; Media Researcher: Rebekah Hubstenberger; Production Specialist: Whitney Schaefer

Image Credits
Alamy: ClassicStock, 29, Pictorial Press Ltd, 16, World History Archive, 19; Bridgeman Images: © Look and Learn, 21; Getty Images: Dorling Kindersley, 14, duncan1890, 4, 25, Hulton Archive, Cover, 6, 10, 26, iStock/joecicak, 18, powerofforever, 9, whitemay, 15; Shutterstock: Apostrophe, design element (texture), cynoclub, 27 (bottom right), Jim Lambert, 23, Ramziya Khusnullina, design element (icons), Wham Arena, 27 (middle right); The Metropolitan Museum of Art: Gift of Louis K. and Susan Pear Meisel, 1985, 7, The Jefferson R. Burdick Collection, Gift of Jefferson R. Burdick, 17; The New York Public Library: Rare Book Division, 13

All internet sites appearing in back matter were available and accurate when this book was sent to press.

TABLE OF CONTENTS

Words in **bold** are in the glossary.

The Lives of Pirates

They are criminals and thieves. Yet for hundreds of years, pirates have captured people's interest.

The Golden Age of Piracy lasted from about 1690 to 1730. Thousands of pirates roamed the seas. Some of the most famous pirates lived during this time.

Not everything people believe about pirates is true. There are many stories told about pirates in books, movies, and TV shows. The way they are shown is often made-up. But some stories are based on the lives of real people. Come along and take a dive into the life of pirates. Three pieces of information will be presented. One of them is a myth or **misconception**. Can you catch what is true and what is a myth?

When attacking other ships, pirates often got into violent battles.

HOW CAN I TELL WHAT'S TRUTH AND WHAT'S A MYTH?

START HERE. ⇨ Does the statement include words like "all" or "none"?

YES ⇨ It might be a myth. Words such as "all" or "none" often simplify complicated topics. These statements might not be true.

NO ⇨ Does the statement include specific information, such as names or dates?

YES ⇨ It might be true. Details are important when dealing with facts. The more details a statement provides, the more likely it is to be true.

NO ⇨ It might be a myth. Vague facts without detail might be made up. It's good to question statements that don't include specific details.

Pirate Treasure

TRUTH OR MYTH?

1. PIRATES OFTEN BURIED THE TREASURE THEY CAPTURED TO KEEP IT SAFE.

Pirates sailed the seas and stole goods from other ships. They needed a way to keep what they collected safe. Burying their **loot** in a secret location was one way to do this.

FACT

A highly prized item stolen by English pirates was an atlas that contained maps.

A pirate from Jamaica stands in front of his ship.

2. THE MOST COMMON PIRATE LOOT WAS ORDINARY GOODS USEFUL FOR DAILY LIFE.

Most of the ships traveling the seas were merchant ships. They carried ordinary goods to sell or trade. These included food, lumber, weapons, spices, and **textiles**. In addition to **cargo**, pirates took items needed to keep their ships in good working order. These included ropes, sails, and anchors.

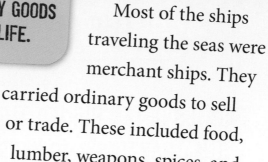

Textiles from the 1700s

3. PIRATES FOLLOWED RULES TO DIVIDE TREASURE IN A FAIR AND ORGANIZED MANNER.

There were usually set rules for how treasure was to be divided among a pirate crew. Those of higher ranks would receive more than sailors with lower ranks. For example, the captain might receive two shares. Crew members might receive one share.

THE MYTH

PIRATES OFTEN BURIED THE TREASURE THEY CAPTURED TO KEEP IT SAFE.

When pirates got their hands on some treasure, they usually spent or used it right away. They couldn't afford to hide it. Burying treasure was also risky. There was no guarantee they would be able to come back for it later, and it could be stolen.

There is one known instance of a pirate burying treasure. Captain William Kidd buried gold and jewels in 1699. He was hoping to come back for the treasure later. But he was arrested in Boston, Massachusetts, and later hanged.

Captain Kidd and his crew buried treasure on Gardiners Island in New York in 1699.

Pirates in Real Life

TRUTH OR MYTH?

1. THE PIRATE KNOWN AS BLACKBEARD WOULD WEAVE HEMP INTO HIS BEARD AND LIGHT IT ON FIRE TO APPEAR ESPECIALLY FRIGHTENING.

Blackbeard

One of history's most well-known pirates is Edward Teach. He is also known as Blackbeard. Blackbeard was known for being especially ruthless. He captured dozens of ships in the early 1700s. At one point, he had three ships and commanded 150 pirates. Blackbeard had a unique way of boosting his fearsome **reputation**. He wrapped slow-burning coils of **hemp** into his beard and lit them on fire.

2. BOYS WERE SOMETIMES PART OF A PIRATE CREW.

Pirate crews sometimes included boys. The boys would usually run errands on the ships. Younger boys worked as powder monkeys. They carried gunpowder from the lower deck to the cannons on the upper deck.

3. ONLY MEN WERE PIRATES. WOMEN WERE NOT ALLOWED BECAUSE THEY WERE CONSIDERED TO BE BAD LUCK ON SHIPS.

Sailors had many **superstitions**. A common one was the belief that women brought bad luck to ships. Pirate crew members refused to allow women to join them. Many men also didn't believe women could do the hard physical work of pirates.

THE MYTH

ONLY MEN WERE PIRATES. WOMEN WERE NOT ALLOWED BECAUSE THEY WERE CONSIDERED TO BE BAD LUCK ON SHIPS.

It was more common for men to be pirates than women. But some women did choose this criminal life. Some women dressed in men's clothing and pretended to be men to join a pirate crew.

But not all women tried to pass as men. One of the most successful women pirates was Zheng Yi Sao. She managed a fleet of more than 70,000 crew members. Grace O'Malley **plundered** ships along the coast of Ireland in the mid-1500s.

Other famous female pirates were Anne Bonny and Mary Read. They sailed with John Rackham in the early 1700s.

Mary Read (left) and
Anne Bonny (right)

FACT

John Rackham was nicknamed Calico Jack.
It came from the cotton clothing that he
often wore. Other pirates often wore silk
and velvet.

Pirate Punishments

TRUTH OR MYTH?

1. MAROONING WAS A PUNISHMENT IN WHICH A CREW WOULD ABANDON A SAILOR ON A DESERTED ISLAND.

One serious punishment was marooning. The crew member would be taken to a deserted island with no food or water and abandoned. They might be given a gun with one shot. The chance of survival was very low.

2. PIRATE CREWS FORCED VICTIMS TO WALK ON A PLANK THAT STUCK OFF THE BOAT AND INTO THE SEA. THEY WERE OFTEN BLINDFOLDED WITH THEIR HANDS TIED.

Many popular stories about pirates describe the practice of walking the plank. This punishment involved hanging a plank off the side of the boat. Victims would be forced to slowly walk out to the end of the plank until they either fell off or jumped.

3. AN ESPECIALLY CRUEL FORM OF PUNISHMENT WAS CALLED KEELHAULING. THE VICTIM WOULD BE TIED TO A LINE AND DRAGGED IN THE WATER BEHIND THE SHIP.

While not used often, keelhauling was a terrible punishment used on pirate ships. A victim was tied to a rope and thrown overboard. Then they were dragged underneath the ship from one side to the other. The result was often fatal.

THE MYTH

PIRATE CREWS FORCED VICTIMS TO WALK ON A PLANK THAT STUCK OFF THE BOAT AND INTO THE SEA. THEY WERE OFTEN BLINDFOLDED WITH THEIR HANDS TIED.

There is not much **evidence** that walking the plank was a real practice. It mostly appears in fictional stories about pirates. This idea may have started in the 1724 book *A General History of the Pyrates*. In it, prisoners were given the option to leave a ship by way of a ladder placed over the water. Of course, it also meant they would have to swim to their freedom.

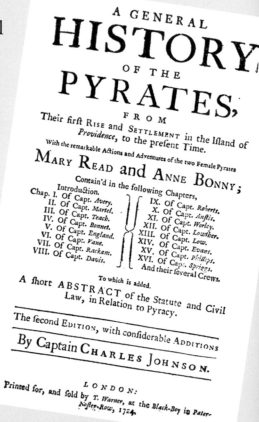

Walking the plank was also featured in other popular stories. Two of the most well known are Robert Louis Stevenson's *Treasure Island* and J. M. Barrie's *Peter Pan*.

Some sources claim the practice was created by Stede Bonnet. He was a pirate from 1717 to 1718. But sources of information about Bonnet are few and unreliable. This claim is not accepted as fact.

Stede Bonnet

Pirate Injuries

1. PIRATES WOULD OFTEN WEAR EYE PATCHES TO COVER UP A MISSING EYE, WHICH WAS SOMETIMES LOST IN FIGHTING.

If pirates lost an eye, they may not have wanted others to see it. So they covered the missing eye with a patch.

2. CREW MEMBERS WOULD BE PAID MONEY IF THEY LOST ANY BODY PARTS.

Many pirate crews paid crew members if they received a serious injury. For example, if a pirate lost their right arm, they might have been paid 600 **pesos**. Payment might have been 500 pesos for a right leg and 100 pesos for a lost finger.

Gold doubloons were coins used during the Golden Age of Piracy.

18

3. REPLACING A LOST LEG WITH A PEG LEG WAS A PRACTICE AMONG PIRATES.

Most pirates who lost a leg probably used crutches to get around. But some used peg legs. These pirates included Francois Le Clerc and Cornelis Corneliszoon Jol. Le Clerc was a pirate in the mid-1500s. He was known as *Jambe de Bois*, a French phrase that means "wooden leg." Jol was nicknamed *Houtebeen*, a Dutch word that also means "wooden leg." He lived from 1597 to 1641.

THE MYTH

PIRATES WOULD OFTEN WEAR EYE PATCHES TO COVER UP A MISSING EYE, WHICH WAS SOMETIMES LOST IN FIGHTING.

It is not known for certain whether pirates actually wore eye patches. But most historians agree eye patches weren't used to cover a missing eye.

Instead, some people believe eye patches were worn to keep one eye adjusted to seeing in the dark. Pirates often needed to move from above deck in the bright sunlight to the darkness of the decks below. By flipping up an eye patch, they could see better in the dark.

Pirate Daily Life

1. PIRATES FOLLOWED STRICT RULES AND A CODE OF CONDUCT TO KEEP ORDER ON THE SHIP.

One might not expect pirates to be good about following rules. But there were codes of honor everyone was expected to follow. The codes set out rules for things such as dividing up loot and assigning chores.

One common rule was no fighting among crew members of the ship. But they could fight once they were on land.

2. PIRATES HAD A SPECIAL WAY OF TALKING AND WOULD SAY THINGS SUCH AS "ARRR!" AND "AHOY, MATEY!"

Pirates had a certain way of speaking. They said phrases such as "Yo ho ho!" and "Shiver me timbers!"

3. ONE OF THE BIGGEST CAUSES OF DEATH ON PIRATE SHIPS WAS A LACK OF VITAMIN C.

It was almost impossible to keep food from rotting and free from pests on a pirate ship. Fresh fruit and vegetables were almost never available.

Without fruits and vegetables, a pirate's diet lacked vitamin C. This would lead to a deadly disease called **scurvy**. Some historians believe scurvy caused more sailor deaths between the late 1400s and the mid-1800s than any other cause.

FACT

Many ships had a curfew for the crew. Pirate captain Bartholomew "Black Bart" Roberts set lights out at 8:00 p.m.

Sailors in the 1700s often ate biscuits called hard tack.

THE MYTH

PIRATES HAD A SPECIAL WAY OF TALKING AND WOULD SAY THINGS SUCH AS "ARRR!" AND "AHOY, MATEY!"

There are many well-known phrases linked to the way pirates talked. But pirates didn't actually talk this way.

The origin of the popular pirate way of speaking was the 1950 Disney movie *Treasure Island*. In it, actor Robert Newton played the fictional pirate character Long John Silver. The movie was based on the 1883 book *Treasure Island* by Robert Louis Stevenson.

Newton came up with the phrases he used in the movie. They included lots of "arrs" as well as "shiver me timbers," "ahoy, me hearties," and the word "landlubbers." Newton based the accent off how people talk in the West Country in southwestern England.

A scene from the book *Treasure Island*

Pirate Ships

TRUTH OR MYTH?

1. PIRATES MOSTLY SAILED ON HUGE SHIPS CALLED GALLEONS.

Stories about pirates often show them sailing on galleons. These huge ships had two or more **masts**. Sailors used the ships in the 1600s and 1700s. They could store a large amount of cargo, and they were armed with cannons. Most galleons could hold hundreds of crew members. Blackbeard sailed a 40-cannon warship called *Queen Anne's Revenge*. Captain Kidd used a 34-cannon ship he named the *Adventure Galley*.

Galleon

2. PIRATE SHIPS OFTEN FLEW A SKULL AND CROSSBONES FLAG.

Pirate crews would fly their own flag called a Jolly Roger. Around the 1700s, most pirates began to use black flags with an image of a skull and crossbones or a skeleton. Some pirates designed their own flags. Blackbeard's flag had a skeleton holding an hourglass, which meant time was running out.

3. PIRATES KEPT PETS ON BOARD, INCLUDING PARROTS.

Life on a pirate ship was often boring. Having a pet helped make daily life more interesting. Parrots made good pets because they were small and didn't need a lot of food. Cats also made good ship pets because they could catch mice and rats. Some experts believe pirates traveling near West Africa and in the Indian Ocean might have had monkeys on board.

THE MYTH

PIRATES MOSTLY SAILED ON HUGE SHIPS CALLED GALLEONS.

Pirates often got their ships by stealing existing ships from someone else. They could trade the ship they had for one they captured. While some famous pirates used large galleons, most pirates used smaller boats. The galleons may have looked impressive, but they were also heavy and slow. Pirates needed boats that were fast enough to catch up with ships. They also needed to quickly escape. Pirates often used boats called schooners. These fast boats often had two masts. But the most popular pirate boats were sloops. These narrow boats were fast and lightweight. They could carry up to 75 pirates and up to a dozen cannons.

FACT

Pirates are still active today. They mostly attack ships around Indonesia, Malaysia, Ghana, and Angola.

Pirates in a small boat try to catch up to a Spanish galleon.

Hundreds of years ago, pirates struck fear into the hearts of merchant ship sailors. From the pirates' lives of plunder came many myths. How many myths did you spot on your journey of the high seas?

GLOSSARY

cargo (KAHR-goh)—the goods carried by a ship

evidence (EH-vuh-duhnss)—information, items, and facts that help prove something to be true or false

loot (LOOT)—stolen money or valuables

hemp (HEMP)—a tall Asian herb

mast (MAST)—a tall pole on a boat's deck that holds its sails

misconception (mis-kuhn-SEP-shuhn)—a wrong or inaccurate idea

peso (PAY-so)—an old silver coin of Spain and Spanish America

plunder (PLUHN-dur)—to steal by force

reputation (reh-pyuh-TAY-shuhn)—a person's character as judged by other people

scurvy (SKUHR-vee)—a deadly disease caused by lack of vitamin C; scurvy produces swollen limbs, bleeding gums, and weakness

superstition (soo-pur-STI-shuhn)—a belief that an action can affect the outcome of a future event

textile (TEK-stile)—a fabric or cloth that has been woven or knitted

READ MORE

Heos, Bridget. *Who Wants to Be a Pirate?: What It Was Really Like in the Golden Age of Piracy.* New York: Henry Holt and Company, 2019.

Hoena, Blake. *Blackbeard: Captain of the Queen Anne's Revenge.* Minneapolis: Bellwether Media, 2021.

Ramsey, Grace. *Pirates.* Vero Beach, FL: Rourke Educational Media, 2019.

INTERNET SITES

DK Findout!: Pirates
dkfindout.com/uk/history/pirates

Kiddle: Piracy Facts for Kids
kids.kiddle.co/Piracy

Pirates of the Caribbean Interactive Map
mrnussbaum.com/pirates-of-the-caribbean-interactive-map

Royal Museums Greenwich: The Golden Age of Piracy
rmg.co.uk/stories/topics/golden-age-piracy

INDEX

ABOUT THE AUTHOR

Carol Kim is the author of several fiction and nonfiction books for kids. She enjoys researching and uncovering little-known facts and sharing what she learns with young readers. Carol lives in Austin, Texas, with her family. Learn more about her and her latest books at her website, CarolKimBooks.com.